Facts About the Goat

By Lisa Strattin

© 2019 Lisa Strattin

Facts for Kids Picture Books by Lisa Strattin

Harlequin Macaw, Vol 34

Downy Woodpecker, Vol 37

Frilled Lizard, Vol 39

Purple Finch, Vol 48

Poison Dart Frogs, Vol 50

Giant Otter, Vol 57

Hornbill, Vol 67

Dwarf Lemur, Vol 73

Giant Squirrel, Vol 76

Star Tortoise, Vol 79

Sign Up for New Release Emails Here

http://LisaStrattin.com/subscribe-here

Monthly Surprise Box

http://KidCraftsByLisa.com

Contents

INTRODUCTION...7

CHARACTERISTICS 9

APPEARANCE...11

LIFE STAGES 13

LIFE SPAN 15

SIZE...17

HABITAT 19

DIET 21

FRIENDS AND ENEMIES 23

SUITABILITY AS PETS...25

PLUSH GOAT TOY 38

MONTHLY SURPRISE BOX..39

INTRODUCTION

Goats originated from the mountainous areas of west Asia and eastern Europe, grazing on hillsides and plains. Modern day common goats are known as domesticated goats and are thought to be very closely related to a sheep.

For thousands of years goats have been used for their meat, hair, milk and skins. In some countries goats are also used to help with carrying heavy loads.

CHARACTERISTICS

One of the rarer species of goat is the fainting goat from Tennessee in the United States. These goats literally freeze up, the goats legs go rigid and the goat falls over. The goat will soon get back up and continue grazing until it happens again. No one seems to know why it happens, but it doesn't seem to hurt them.

The goat is most closely related to the sheep and there are many similarities between the two species, as well as a number of differences, including the tail length of the goat which is noticeably longer than the tail of a sheep.

APPEARANCE

Most species of male goats naturally have two horns on the top of their head. The horns of the goat are made out of the substance keratin, from which human fingernails are also made. The male goats mainly use their horns to defend themselves from other dominant male goats and from unwanted predators. Some species of goat also have females that have two horns on the tops of their heads.

There are any different colors of goats, from white, black, brown and many shades in between. There are also different textures of hair on some goats.

LIFE STAGES

The goat is a mammal, so it gives birth to live babies, called kids. The length of the female's pregnancy is about 150 days. A new kid nurses on its mothers milk until it is ready to start grazing on grasses at around 10 to 12 weeks of age.

It is called a yearling goat once is has passed it first birthday. It is considered a young adult at this time.

However, they are able to mate as early as 4 to 6 months of age!

LIFE SPAN

Goats live, on average, 10 to 15 years!

SIZE

Goats are anywhere from 15 to 31 inches tall and can weigh between 120 and 170 pounds. There are some lighter weight goats, though, like the pygmy and dwarf varieties. These might only be about 80 pounds as adults.

HABITAT

Goats are typically found in more barren landscapes and many species of goat tend to prefer mountainous and rocky terrains. The goats that inhabit mountainous cliff faces are amazingly agile, are able to hold their position well on small ledges and are very adept at jumping and running around on them.

They do live well on farms and ranches, as well as even smaller places where people just want to have them as pets. Even areas less than an acre can be plenty of space for a pet goat to be happy.

DIET

Goats are herbivores who eat grasses, fruits, flowers. leaves, and grains. You can even buy goat feed at many farmer supply stores.

FRIENDS AND ENEMIES

The goat is natural prey to many predators which include leopards, tigers, large reptiles and most commonly humans. Today the goat is also found in parts of South America where the goats are farmed and hunted for their meat and skins.

SUITABILITY AS PETS

Goats can be very good pets. Although they are known to sometimes head butt their human owners, they are entertaining to watch and a lot of fun to have around. They are friendly and like to be petted, just like dogs and cats do. You probably don't want one in your house, but if you have a nice space for them, they are easy to keep as a pet.

COLOR ME

COLOR ME

COLOR ME

COLOR ME

COLOR ME

COLOR ME

Please leave me a review here:

http://lisastrattin.com/Review-Vol-181

For more Kindle Downloads Visit Lisa Strattin Author Page on Amazon Author Central

http://amazon.com/author/lisastrattin

To see upcoming titles, visit my website at LisaStrattin.com– all books available on kindle!

http://lisastrattin.com

PLUSH GOAT TOY

You can get one by copying and pasting this link into your browser:

http://lisastrattin.com/PlushGoatToy

MONTHLY SURPRISE BOX

Get yours by copying and pasting this link into your browser

http://KidCraftsByLisa.com

Made in the USA
Middletown, DE
04 July 2022